W9-CYH-424

Petits Fours

THE FINISHING TOUCH

Petits Fours

AARON MAREE

Angus&Robertson
An imprint of HarperCollins*Publishers*

*To the many friends who have helped
with research and recipe testing,
and who have given me moral support.*

AN ANGUS & ROBERTSON BOOK
An imprint of HarperCollinsPublishers

First published in Australia in 1993 by
CollinsAngus&Robertson Publishers Pty Limited
A division of HarperCollinsPublishers (Australia) Pty Limited
25 Ryde Road, Pymble NSW 2073, Australia

HarperCollinsPublishers (New Zealand) Limited
31 View Road, Glenfield, Auckland 10, New Zealand

HarperCollinsPublishers Limited
77-85 Fulham Palace Road, London W6 8JB, United Kingdom

Distributed in the United States of America by
HarperCollinsPublishers
10 East 53rd Street, New York NY 10022, USA

Copyright © Aaron Maree 1993

This book is copyright.
Apart from any fair dealing for the purposes of private study,
research, criticism or review, as permitted under the Copyright
Act, no part may be reproduced by any process without written
permission. Inquiries should be addressed to the publishers.

National Library of Australia
Cataloguing-in-Publication data:

Maree Aaron.
  Petits fours.

  Includes index.
  ISBN 0 207 18035 0.

  1. Cake. I. Title (Series: Finishing touch).

641.8653

Photographer: Andre Martin
Stylist: Karen Carter
Assistant Stylist: Katie Mitchell

Printed in the People's Republic of China

5 4 3 2 1
96 95 94 93

Contents

Petit Four Glacé

CHAPTER ONE

Cake-based

Petits fours are the finale of the dining experience.
They are traditionally served after dessert with coffee.
Petit four is a French term that literally means 'small
oven', and refers to small cakes and biscuits which are
often iced and decorated. These tiny delicacies were
originally baked in small ovens by the specialist pastry
chefs of France.

◆

There are two kinds of petits fours: Petit Four 'Sec',
meaning 'dry', and Petit Four 'Glacé', meaning 'iced'.
Thus, Petit Four Sec is a biscuit or pastry-based petit
four and Petit Four Glacé is an iced or glazed petit four.
Cake-based petits fours can be either Petit Four 'Sec' or
'Glacé' depending on their finish or filling.

Petit Four Glacé — Basic Recipe

◆

75 g (2 ½ oz) unsalted butter, softened
¼ cup (2 oz) caster (superfine) sugar
3 egg yolks
5 teaspoons (1 oz) caster (superfine) sugar
6 egg whites
⅔ cup (2 ½ oz) plain (all-purpose) flour, sifted
extra caster (superfine) sugar, for sprinkling
⅓ cup (4 oz) apricot jam
120 g (4 oz) plain marzipan (see p. 61)

Preheat oven to 160°C (320°F). Line four 18 x 28 x 2 cm (7 x 11 x ¾ in) baking trays (sheets) with baking parchment.

Place the butter and the first amount of sugar into a mixing bowl and cream together until light and fluffy. Add the egg yolks one at a time and continue creaming the mixture until a smooth and light consistency is achieved. In a separate bowl, whisk the egg whites until they form stiff peaks. Gradually add the second amount of the sugar and whisk until combined. Fold the flour through the whisked egg whites, then fold the egg white mixture lightly through the butter mixture until completely incorporated. Spread this mixture thinly between the prepared trays. Bake each tray (or if you can fit them, all the trays together) for 12–15 minutes or until the sponge mixture is a light golden brown. Remove from the oven and sprinkle each cake sheet with caster sugar before turning out on to sheets of baking parchment. (By sprinkling this extra sugar on top you will prevent the cake sheets from sticking to the baking parchment.)

Once cooled, remove the baking parchment from both sides of the cake layers. Place one cake layer on the work surface and spread thinly with apricot jam. Place the second cake layer on top of the first and spread it with jam. Repeat for remaining layers. Place the layered sponge into a baking tray lined with greaseproof (waxed) paper. Place another sheet of greaseproof paper on top. Weigh down the sponge using a chopping board with a brick (or cans of food) wrapped in aluminium foil placed on top. Leave in the refrigerator for several hours or preferably overnight.

Remove the brick (or can), chopping board and paper from the layered sponge. On a lightly floured surface roll the marzipan into a thin sheet. Spread the top of the layered sponge sparingly with apricot jam, then place the rolled marzipan on top. Press the marzipan down firmly to ensure there are no air bubbles. Turn the whole lot over so that the marzipan is face

down and, using a ruler and a knife
or different shaped cutters, cut the
layered sponge into small-sized
portons which are not bigger than
3 x 3 cm (1 x 1 in). (Cutting the
layered sponge marzipan-side down
will ensure clean edges for the
finished petits fours.) Leave the
cut pieces marzipan-side down
and prepare the fondant glaze.

*1. Weigh down the jam-spread sponge layers
using a chopping board with a brick wrapped
in aluminium foil placed on top.*

*2. Cut out small-sized portions from the sponge
(the marzipan is at the bottom).*

*3. Insert a fork into the base of the upturned
petit four and dip it into the fondant.*

*4. Decorate the dry petits fours with chocolate
piping designs.*

FONDANT DIPPING

Fondant can be bought commercially
in small tubs and packets from
supermarkets or it can be bought in
large quantities from bakeries. You
will need 300 g (10 ½ oz) of fondant
to glaze the petits fours. For the
fondant dipping of petits fours the
fondant is heated over a water bath
(bain marie or double broiler) to
between 35°C (95°F) and 37°C
(99°F), no hotter. Overheating the
fondant will result in the sugar

crystallising and will give a patchy look to the glaze when set. As the fondant heats, add any flavourings or colourings, then thin it down with water to the required consistency. Stir the fondant constantly while heating to give a fuller sheen to it when set. The petits fours are now ready to be coated with the fondant.

COATING PETITS FOURS

There are many ways of coating petits fours and as you experiment you will find your own favourite way.

One way is to buy a dipping fork from a specialist kitchenware store. Insert the fork into the base of the petit four. Then dip the petit four into the warm thin fondant and turn right side up to dry on the wire cooling rack.

The second and cheaper way is to pick up the petit four by the base using your fingers, dip it into the fondant and then turn it right side up to drain and dry. Excess fondant will run off the sides of the dipped petit four and can be remelted and used again with fresh fondant as long as it is free from cake crumbs.

It is a good practice to dip just one or two petits fours and to let them set before dipping all of them. This will tell you if the consistency of your fondant is correct. A correct fondant glaze should be thin enough to drain away from the top of the petit four and leave a bevelled edge, letting each of the layers show through. The fondant will take approximately 5–10 minutes to dry. If the fondant does not look dry allow it to set a few minutes longer. Once the fondant is bruised or cracked or has fingerprints on it the whole petit four is ruined.

When you are certain that the fondant has set, carefully slide a flat sharp knife under each petit four, separating it from the rack and removing all excess fondant. To prevent the now exposed underside of the petit four from drying out, place it into a paper petit four cup to give it a protective seal. Decorate with chocolate piping designs (see p. 62).

Makes 20–24

Chocolate Honey Bernhardts

◆

As the filling needs refrigeration for 12 hours, make it first.

½ cup (6 oz) clear honey
2 tablespoons (2 oz) golden syrup
30 g (1 oz) unsalted butter
2 tablespoons (2 oz) walnut oil
½ cup (4 oz) caster (superfine) sugar
3 ¼ cups (14 oz) plain (all-purpose)
flour
1 tablespoon ground cinnamon
½ tablespoon (⅕ oz) baking powder
1 ⅓ cups (5 oz) ground hazelnuts
2 eggs

FILLING
440 ml (15 ½ fl oz) thickened (double
or heavy) cream
½ cup (3 oz) icing (powdered) sugar
120 g (4 oz) unsalted butter
240 g (8 ½ oz) milk chocolate, chopped

375 g (13 oz) dark (plain or semi-
sweet) chocolate, melted
extra icing (powdered) sugar, for
dusting

Grease and line a 25 x 30 x 3 cm
(10 x 12 x 1 in) baking tray (sheet)
with baking parchment.

Place the honey, syrup, butter, oil
and sugar into a saucepan and bring
the mixture to the boil, stirring
occasionally to ensure the mixture
does not burn. Boil for two minutes.
Remove and cool. Sift the flour,
cinnamon and baking powder into a
bowl with the ground hazelnuts and
the lightly beaten eggs. Add the
cooled butter and honey mixture and
work with a wooden spoon until the
mixture forms a dough. Remove from
the bowl and knead lightly. Press the
mixture evenly into the prepared tray
and place the tray in the refrigerator
for 1 hour. Preheat oven to 180°C
(350°F).

After one hour remove tray from
refrigerator and bake for 30–35
minutes. Remove when baked and
cool in tray.

Using a 4 cm (1 ½ in) plain round
cookie cutter, cut discs from the
cooled cake base and set aside.

Place the chilled filling into the
mixing bowl and whisk until light
and airy.

Using a piping (pastry) bag fitted
with a 1 cm (⅓ in) plain round
nozzle, pipe the filling into peaks on
top of each cake disc. Place the decorated discs into the freezer to firm.
After 30 minutes remove discs and
dip the top of each one into the
melted chocolate only as far as the
top of the cake base. Turn upright
so that the chocolate drips down
over the cake base while it is setting.
Allow to set before dusting lightly
with icing sugar.

Chocolate Honey Bernhardts

FILLING

Place the cream, icing sugar and butter into a saucepan and bring to the boil. Remove from the heat and stir in the chopped chocolate. Stir till well combined before refrigerating for 12 hours or overnight.

Makes 12–18

3. *Dip the firm Bernhardts into the melted chocolate as far as the top of the cake base.*

1. *Cut discs from the cooled cake base with a round cookie cutter.*

2. *Carefully pipe the filling mixture into peaks on each cake disc.*

Chocolate Orange Madeleines

◆

Make sure you use the rose-water in this recipe as it is the essence of a madeleine.

150 g (5 oz) unsalted butter, softened
1 ¼ cups (7 ½ oz) icing (powdered) sugar, sifted
3 eggs
1 ½ cups (6 oz) plain (all-purpose) flour, sifted
2 tablespoons (½ oz) cocoa powder, sifted
1 teaspoon baking powder
1 tablespoon orange juice, freshly squeezed
1 teaspoon rose-water
rind of 1 orange, finely grated
extra icing (powdered) sugar, for dusting

Preheat oven to 180°C (350°F). Lightly grease a madeleine tray.

Cream the unsalted butter and sifted icing sugar until they are light and fluffy. Add the eggs, one at a time, to the creamed mix and combine well. Add the plain sifted flour, cocoa powder and baking powder to the mixture with the freshly squeezed orange juice, rose-water and orange rind. Mix until all ingredients are completely blended. Place the mixture into the madeleine moulds so that they are three-quarters full.

Bake in the preheated oven 15–20 minutes or until each madeleine is springy to touch. When baked, turn out immediately and dust lightly with icing sugar before serving warm.

Makes 24

Toscanner (above), Chocolate Orange Madeleines (left), Othellos (right)

Othellos

5 egg yolks
¾ cup (3 ½ oz) plain (all-purpose) flour
160 ml (5 ½ fl oz) water
5 egg whites
⅓ cup (3 oz) caster (superfine) sugar
2/3 cup (2 ½ oz) cornflour
(US cornstarch)
120 g (4 oz) apricot jam
icing (powdered) sugar, for dusting

Preheat oven to 160°C (320°F).
Grease and lightly flour three baking
trays (sheets).

Place the egg yolks, flour and
water in an electric mixer and beat at
top speed for 15–20 minutes to make
the mixture light and airy.

In a separate bowl, beat the egg
whites until stiff peaks form and then
beat in the sugar, a spoonful at a
time, until it is all dissolved. Gently
fold in the cornflour by hand. Take a
spoonful of the egg white mixture and
mix, by hand, into the egg yolk mixture. Gently fold the remaining egg
whites into the egg yolk mixture.
Pour the mixture into a piping
(pastry) bag fitted with a ½ cm (¼ in)
plain round nozzle. Pipe small domes
of mixture of approximately 4 cm
(1 ½ in) in diameter on to the greased
trays.

Bake each tray for 12–15 minutes, until each Othello is a light
golden brown and springy to touch.
Allow the Othellos to cool on the
trays. When cool, pair them up so
that two of the same shape and size
fit together. Spread apricot jam on
to the flat side of one of the Othellos
and join two together. Dust lightly
with icing sugar before serving.

Makes 24–30

Toscanner

1 ¼ cups (5 oz) plain (all-purpose) flour
⅓ cup (2 oz) icing (powdered) sugar
90 g (3 oz) unsalted butter
1 egg
1 tablespoon cold water

FILLING
150 g (5 oz) unsalted butter
⅔ cup (5 oz) caster (superfine) sugar
1 egg
⅓ cup (1 ½ oz) plain (all-purpose) flour,
sifted
1 ⅓ cups (5 oz) ground almonds

TOPPING
55 g (2 oz) unsalted butter
1/4 cup (2 oz) caster (superfine) sugar
1 tablespoon (1 oz) clear honey
½ cup (2 oz) slivered almonds

300 g (10 ½ oz) dark (plain or
semi-sweet) chocolate, melted

Preheat oven to 180°C (350°F).
Grease and line a 25 x 30 x 3 cm
(10 x 12 x 1 in) baking tray (sheet)
with baking parchment.

Place the flour and icing sugar in a
bowl and very lightly rub in the butter
until the mixture resembles coarse
breadcrumbs. Add the egg and water
and work to a firm dough. Press the
dough into the prepared tray with
lightly floured hands.

Spread the filling over the pastry-
lined tray and bake for 35–40 minutes or until brown and firm to the
touch. Allow to cool in the tray.

Using a lightly oiled palette knife,
spread the topping mixture over the
baked base. Return the whole slice,
in its tray, to the oven for 15 minutes, then cool and refrigerate overnight. Cut the slice into squares and
dip each square into the melted
chocolate. Dip the squares so that
only the praline topping is not
covered with chocolate.

FILLING
Place the butter and sugar into a
mixing bowl and beat until creamy,
light and fluffy. Add the egg and beat
for 3 minutes. Beat in the sifted flour
and ground almonds.

TOPPING
Place all the topping ingredients into
a saucepan and slowly bring to the
boil. Boil for 2 minutes or until the
mixture begins to leave the sides of
the pan.

Makes 40–48

Kirsch Tartlets

CHAPTER TWO

Biscuit-based

*Like cake-based petits fours, these delicious tiny treats
can either be Petit Four 'Sec' — biscuit-based and
sometimes filled with cream or chocolate — or Petit Four
'Glacé' — iced and decorated. The filling of these petits
fours is often flavoured with liqueur or coffee.*

◆

*Biscuit-based petits fours are traditionally served after
the final course with coffee. They can even be served for
afternoon tea. They really provide that 'finishing touch'
to any occasion.*

Kirsch Tartlets

¾ cup (3 ½ oz) plain (all-purpose) flour
3 tablespoons (1 ½ oz) icing (powdered)
sugar
75 g (2 ½ oz) unsalted butter
1 egg yolk
180 g (6 oz) plain marzipan coloured
with 2–3 drops red (cochineal) food
colouring (for marzipan see p. 61)
90 g (3 oz) white chocolate, melted
10 whole glacé (candied) cherries,
halved

FILLING

180 g (6 oz) unsalted butter
½ cup (3 oz) icing (powdered)
sugar
1 egg
few drops of vanilla essence (extract)
1 tablespoon Kirsch liqueur
2 tablespoons glacé (candied) cherries,
finely chopped

Preheat oven to 180°C (350°F).
Lightly grease a tartlet pan (18–24
moulds).

Sift the flour and icing sugar into
a bowl. Add the butter and lightly rub
through the dry ingredients until the
mixture resembles fine breadcrumbs.

Add the egg yolk and continue mixing until a dough is formed. Wrap
the dough in plastic (cling) wrap and
refrigerate until firm.

Remove the dough and knead
lightly until pliable. On a lightly
floured surface roll the dough to
2 mm thick and, using a 2–3 cm
(¾–1 in) round plain cookie cutter,
cut out 18–24 discs. Place each disc
into the tartlet moulds and press in
firmly. Bake in the preheated oven
12 minutes, then allow tartlets to
cool in their moulds. Fill the tartlet
shells with the kirsch filling making
sure the tops are level. Roll out the
marzipan on a lightly floured surface
and cut out discs the same size as the
top of the tartlets. Place one disc on
top of each tartlet. Pipe a dot of
melted white chocolate on top of
each tartlet and place a halved cherry
on top of this.

FILLING

Place the butter and icing sugar into
a mixing bowl and cream together
until light and fluffy. Add the egg,
vanilla and Kirsch and beat into the
butter and icing sugar until well
combined. Add the glacé cherries.

Makes 18–24

1. Fill each tartlet shell with the Kirsch cream, making sure the tops are level.

2. Roll the marzipan thinly and cut out discs the same size as each tartlet.

Langue de Chat

◆

165 g (6 oz) unsalted butter, softened
1 ¼ cups (7 ½ oz) icing (powdered)
sugar, sifted
4 egg whites
¼ cup (2 oz) caster (superfine) sugar
1 ¼ cups (5 ½ oz) plain
(all-purpose) flour, sifted

Preheat oven to 200°C (400°F) and line a baking tray (sheet) with baking parchment.

Place the butter and icing sugar into a mixing bowl and cream together until light, fluffy and almost white. In a separate bowl, whisk the egg whites until they form stiff peaks. As they stiffen, gradually add the caster sugar. Continue whisking after each addition of caster sugar. Fold the stiff egg whites into the creamed butter mixture, then fold through the flour.

Place the mixture into a piping (pastry) bag fitted with a 1 cm (⅓ in) round piping nozzle and pipe 7 cm (2 ¾ in) lengths on to the prepared tray, leaving plenty of room between each for spreading.

Bake in the preheated oven 5–8 minutes. Remove from the oven and cool on the tray for 5 minutes before placing on a wire cooling rack.

Makes 36

Coconut Macaroons

◆

2 ⅓ cups (10 ½ oz) desiccated
(shredded) coconut
2 cups (16 oz) caster (superfine) sugar
9 egg whites
juice of 1 lemon
300 g (10 ½ oz) dark (plain or
semi-sweet) chocolate, melted

Preheat oven to 180°C (350°F) and line a baking tray (sheet) with baking parchment.

Place the coconut and sugar into a large saucepan and stir lightly with a wooden spoon. Add the egg whites and lemon juice and stir the mixture to a moist paste. Place the saucepan over a low heat and continue to stir until the mixture reaches 40°C (104°F) on a sugar (candy) thermometer. Remove the pan from the heat and continue stirring until the mixture cools. Place the mixture into a piping (pastry) bag which has been fitted with a 1 ½ cm (½ in) star piping nozzle. Pipe the mixture into rosette shapes on the baking tray, leaving 1–2 cm (⅓ – ¾ in) between each. Bake for 10–15 minutes or until the mixture is just beyond golden brown. Cool on the tray before dipping the bases into chocolate. Allow the chocolate to set before serving.

Makes 36

Langue de Chat (above), Coconut Macaroons (below)

Mocha Fancies

Mocha Fancies

◆

¾ cup (3 oz) plain (all-purpose) flour
2 tablespoons (½ oz) cocoa powder
1 teaspoon instant coffee granules
3 tablespoons (1 ½ oz) icing
(powdered) sugar
75 g (2 ½ oz) unsalted butter
1 egg

MOCHA GANACHE
150 ml (5 fl oz) thickened (double
or heavy) cream
1 teaspoon instant coffee granules
300 g (10 ½ oz) dark (plain or
semi-sweet) chocolate, melted

ICING GLAZE
2 tablespoons warm water
1 teaspoon instant coffee granules
1 cup (6 oz) icing (powdered) sugar

90 g (3 oz) dark (plain or semi-sweet)
chocolate, melted, for decoration

Preheat oven to 180°C (350°F).
Grease a tartlet pan (18–24 moulds).
Sift together the flour, cocoa powder,
coffee granules and the icing sugar
and place in a bowl. Rub the butter
into the dry ingredients until the
mixture resembles coarse breadcrumbs. Add the egg and continue
mixing until a dough is formed. Wrap
the dough in plastic (cling) wrap and
refrigerate until firm. Remove the
dough and knead lightly until it is
pliable enough to roll.

On a lightly floured surface, roll
the dough to 2 mm or as thinly as
possible. Using a 2–3 cm (¾–1 in)
plain round cookie cutter, cut out
discs from the rolled dough. Place
each disc into the prepared tartlet
pan. Bake in the preheated oven
10–12 minutes. Remove from the
oven and allow to cool in the pan.
Remove each baked tartlet shell from
its mould and fill with the cooling
ganache. Fill so that the top of the
ganache is level with the top of the
tartlet shell. Place each filled tartlet
shell on to a tray. When the tray is
full put into the freezer until the
filling is firm. Remove and cover the
top of each Mocha Fancy with a little
icing. Dot the top of each with a little
melted chocolate before serving.

MOCHA GANACHE
Place the cream and coffee granules
into a saucepan and allow to come to
the boil. Remove the saucepan from
the heat and add the melted chocolate, stirring until the mix is thick
and smooth. Allow to cool slightly.

ICING GLAZE
Combine the water and coffee. Add
enough of the coffee mix to the icing
sugar to form a thick but spreadable
paste when mixed together. If the
icing is too thick add warm water, a
teaspoon at a time. If it is too runny
add teaspoons of icing sugar until you
get the correct consistency.

Makes 18–24

Brandy Snaps

¾ cup (6 oz) caster (superfine) sugar
½ cup (6 oz) golden syrup (dark
corn syrup)
90 g (3 oz) unsalted butter
¾ cup (3 oz) plain (all-purpose) flour

Place the sugar, golden syrup and butter into a saucepan and place over a low heat. Allow the butter to melt and mix into the other ingredients but do not allow the mixture to boil. When all ingredients are melted into a syrup, remove from the heat. Add the flour and stir with a wooden spoon until combined. Pour into a container and refrigerate for 1–2 hours or until mixture is quite cool and firm.

Lightly grease several baking trays (sheets) and preheat oven to 180°C (350°F).

Take a teaspoonful of the chilled mixture at a time and roll into small balls. Place each ball on to the tray at regular intervals, leaving plenty of room between each for spreading. When the tray is full, dip your fingers into cold water and flatten the balls out. Bake in the preheated oven 5–8 minutes or until the Brandy Snaps are bubbling and slightly coloured.

Remove the tray from the oven and allow to cool slightly before attempting to remove the Brandy Snaps. When they have firmed slightly, peel them carefully from the tray, using a knife and spatula and roll each one quickly around the handle of a wooden spoon. You can probably mould 2 or 3 at a time on the wooden spoon. If the Brandy Snaps harden while they are waiting to be moulded, place them back into the oven for a few minutes to soften. Allow to cool around the mould. When cool, slide from the mould and either leave plain or fill with freshly whipped cream.

Makes 24–36

Brandy Snaps

Almond Tuiles

¾ cup (4 oz) icing (powdered) sugar
1 cup (4 oz) plain (all-purpose) flour
3 egg whites
90 g (3 oz) unsalted butter,
melted
1 ⅓ cups (5 oz) slivered almonds,
for garnish

Preheat oven to 180°C (350°F).
Lightly grease two baking trays
(sheets).

Sift the icing sugar and flour into
a bowl, then add the lightly whisked
egg whites. Stir until well mixed.
Allow the mixture to sit uncovered
for 5–10 minutes. Pour the melted
butter over the top of the mixture
and stir until a smooth paste forms.
Allow mixture to rest for a further
5 minutes.

Take a tablespoonful of the mixture and place it on to the prepared
tray, spreading into a large circle,
using the back of a spoon. Spread the
mixture very thinly and sprinkle a few
slivered almonds on top of each tuile.
Bake in the preheated oven 8–10
minutes or until the tuiles are just
turning golden brown around the
edges. Remove the tray from the
oven and use a clean palette knife
or spatula to carefully and quickly
remove each tuile before it sets hard.
Drape each tuile over a rolling pin or
any utensil that will give the biscuit a
curved shape. Allow the tuiles to cool
over the rolling pin, then store them
in an airtight container.
Note: These petits fours are best
made the day required as they will
soften quickly and lose their shape
if not eaten immediately.

Makes 18–24

Pineapple Delights

◆

¾ cup (3 ½ oz) plain (all-purpose)
flour
3 tablespoons (1 ½ oz) icing
(powdered) sugar
75 g (2 ½ oz) unsalted butter
1 egg yolk
1 ¾ cups (7 ½ oz) glacé (candied)
pineapple, finely chopped
150 g (5 oz) pink-coloured marzipan or
white marzipan coloured with 2–3
drops red (cochineal) colouring
(for marzipan see p. 61)
90 g (3 oz) white chocolate, melted
¾ cup (3 oz) glacé (candied) pineapple,
for decoration

Preheat oven to 180°C (350°F).
Lightly grease a tartlet pan (18–24
moulds).

Sift together the flour and icing
sugar and place into a bowl. Add the
butter and lightly rub through the dry
ingredients until the mixture resembles fine breadcrumbs. Add the egg
yolk and continue mixing until a

dough is formed. Wrap the dough in
plastic (cling) wrap and refrigerate
until firm. Remove the dough and
knead lightly until pliable. On a
lightly floured surface roll the dough
to 2–3 mm or as thinly as possible.
Using a 2–3 cm (¾–1 in) round plain
cookie cutter, cut out 18–24 discs.
Place each disc into a tartlet mould
and press in firmly.

Bake in the preheated oven 12
minutes and then allow discs to cool
in their tartlet moulds.

When cool remove the tartlets
from the pan and fill them with the
glacé (candied) pineapple. Roll the
pink-coloured marzipan to 2 mm
thick or as thinly as possible. Using
fluted round cookie cutters, cut out
discs which are large enough to cover
the top of each tartlet shell when full.

Place the marzipan on top of each
filled tartlet and in the centre of the
marzipan place a dot of melted white
chocolate. On top of that place a
sliver of the remaining glacé (candied)
pineapple.

Makes 18–24

Almond Tuiles (above), Pineapple Delights (left), Praline Tartlets (right)

Praline Tartlets

◆

¾ cup (3 ½ oz) plain (all-purpose) flour
3 tablespoons (1 ½ oz) icing (powdered)
sugar
75 g (2 ½ oz) unsalted butter
1 egg yolk

PRALINE GANACHE FILLING
150 ml (5 fl oz) thickened (double
or heavy) cream
300 g (10 ½ oz) dark (plain or
semi-sweet) chocolate, melted
¾ cup (4 oz) praline, crushed
(see recipe below)

PRALINE
⅔ cup (5 oz) white granulated sugar
½ cup (2 oz) slivered almonds

extra icing (powdered) sugar, for
dusting

Preheat oven to 180°C (350°F).
Lightly grease a tartlet pan (18–24
moulds). Sift the flour and icing
sugar into a bowl. Add the butter and
rub through the dry ingredients until
they resemble breadcrumbs. Add the
egg yolk and mix until a dough is
formed. Wrap the dough in plastic
(cling) wrap and refrigerate until firm.
Remove from the refrigerator and
knead the dough lightly to make it
pliable. Roll out on a lightly floured
surface as thinly as possible and,
using a 2–3 cm (¾–1 in) plain round
cookie cutter, cut discs from the
dough. Press each disc into the
prepared tartlet case. Bake the tartlet
cases together for 12 minutes and
allow tartlets to cool in their cases.

Fill each tartlet case with praline
ganache. Pipe into the tartlet case
using a piping (pastry) bag if the
mixture is too thick to spoon in.
When the tartlets are filled, dip the
tops into the remaining crushed
praline and dust lightly with icing
sugar before serving.

PRALINE GANACHE FILLING
Place the cream into a saucepan and
bring to the boil. Remove from heat.
Add the melted chocolate and stir
until the mixture is smooth and
thick. Allow mix to cool slightly
before placing into the refrigerator.
Stir it occasionally until it becomes
quite thick. Remove from refrigerator. Add the finely crushed praline
and stir through. Reserve remaining
praline for decoration.

PRALINE
Place the sugar into a saucepan over a
high heat and stir continually. When
all the sugar has melted and a smooth
brown liquid has formed remove the
saucepan from the heat and add the
slivered almonds. Stir until well combined, then pour the mixture on to a
lightly oiled marble slab, stainless
steel bench (counter) top or sheet of
foil. Spread thinly and allow to cool.
Once cool, the mixture will be very
hard. Place inside a strong plastic bag
and, using a rolling pin, crush the
praline until it breaks into very small
pieces. Store in the bag in an airtight
container until required.

Makes 18–24

Flame Baked Squares (left), Almond Horns (right)

CHAPTER THREE

Marzipan-based

Marzipan is the perfect medium to use for petits fours — it not only tastes delicious, it is also easy to model into animals and novelty shapes, use in recipes for baking and make into individual marzipan treats.

◆

There are many different theories on where marzipan originated. Some say it was originally produced by an order of nuns, others say that famine in Europe led to the usage of almonds and sugar to make a substance resembling bread. Regardless of the confusion about its origins, marzipan is now enjoyed by petit four lovers' around the world.

Almond Horns

540 g (19 oz) plain marzipan
(see p. 61)
1 ¼ cups (10 ½ oz) white
granulated sugar
4 egg whites
2 ¼ cups (8 ½ oz) slivered almonds
210 g (7 ½ oz) dark (plain or
semi-sweet) chocolate, melted

Preheat oven to 180°C (350°F).
Prepare a flat baking tray (sheet) by
lining it with a single sheet of baking
parchment.

Place the marzipan and sugar in a
bowl and mix together until they
form a solid mass. Slowly add the egg
whites until a stiff piping consistency
is achieved. This may take more or
less of the stated amount of egg white
in the recipe, depending on the brand
of marzipan used. When the mixture
is ready (better too stiff than too wet),
take tablespoons of the mixture and
roll each into the slivered almonds on
a flat surface until you form a sausage
shape. Place on to the prepared tray.

Bake in the preheated oven 8–10
minutes or until golden brown. Allow
to cool on the tray. When cool, dip
the bases into the melted chocolate
and allow to set on baking parchment
before serving.

Note: Some alternatives to dipping
the bases in melted chocolate are to
leave them plain or drizzle with
chocolate or royal icing.

Makes 18–24

Flame Baked Squares

plain (all-purpose) flour, for dusting
250 g (9 oz) plain marzipan
(for marzipan see p. 61)
1 ½ cups (9 oz) icing (powdered) sugar,
sifted
1–2 egg whites, lightly beaten
⅓ cup (4 oz) strawberry or
apricot jam

Line a baking tray (sheet) with baking parchment which is lightly dusted with plain flour.

Put the marzipan in a mixing bowl and break into very small pieces. Add the sifted icing sugar and crumb the two ingredients together. Add a very small amount of the egg white and mix through. Continue adding egg white by the teaspoon and mix through until a solid dough is formed.

Make certain that the mixture is very stiff but pliable enough to be rolled. Cover the dough and allow to rest for 5 minutes.

On a flat surface, lightly dusted with icing sugar, roll the marzipan dough to 2 cm (¾ in) thick. Place the dough on the prepared tray. Use a ruler to mark the rolled dough into 3 x 3 cm (1 x 1 in) squares. Do not cut the squares completely. Instead use a sharp knife to score the top of the dough through to a depth of 1 cm (⅓ in). Into the centre of each marked square, press into the dough a decorative shape, using the point of a piping (pastry) nozzle, small cutter or any implement that will leave a shallow impression. Allow the sheet of marzipan to sit in a cold oven overnight (12 hours).

Remove the marzipan from the oven and place under a heated grill. Continually turn the marzipan sheet until the top and bottom are evenly but lightly brown. Allow the marzipan to cool for 2 hours before cutting with a sharp knife into the marked squares. Fill each impression with piped jam.

Note: Left in the open air marzipan will form a skin because of its high sugar ratio. While this is undesirable for the majority of petits fours, this reaction to the air can be put to good use in the making of flame baked goods as it gives them a delightful and decorative finish.

Makes 18–24

Macaroon Mushrooms

◆

3 egg whites
¼ cup (2 oz) caster (superfine) sugar
1 cup (8 oz) caster (superfine) sugar
2 cups (8 oz) ground almonds
400 g (14 oz) plain marzipan
(see p. 61)

90 g (3 oz) dark (plain or semi-sweet)
chocolate, melted, to decorate
90 g (3 oz) white chocolate, melted,
to decorate

Preheat oven to 160°C (320°F). Line a baking tray (sheet) with baking parchment.

Whisk the egg whites and the first amount of sugar until it forms stiff peaks. Place the second amount of the sugar and the ground almonds into a blender and blend together. Continue whisking the egg whites and slowly add the sugar and almonds until all the ingredients are mixed. Using a 1 cm (⅓ in) plain round nozzle, fitted to a piping (pastry) bag, pipe small dots of the mixture, 3–4 cm (1–1 ½ in) in diameter, on to the prepared tray.

Bake in the preheated oven 10–12 minutes or until lightly golden. Allow to cool on the tray. When the biscuits have cooled, take 20 g (¾ oz) amounts of the marzipan and roll them into pear-shaped pieces. Place one almond biscuit on top of the pointed end of the pear shape to complete the mushroom. Eyes and facial features can be piped on with a little melted chocolate or pressed into the marzipan using a knife.

Makes 18–24

Macaroon Mushrooms

Liqueur Squares

Liqueur Squares

◆

*300 g (10 ½ oz) plain marzipan
(for marzipan see p. 61)
¾ cup (4 oz) icing (powdered)
sugar
rind of 1 orange, finely grated
15 ml (½ fl oz) Grand Marnier
1 egg white (if needed)
210 g (7 ½ oz) dark (plain or
semi-sweet) chocolate, melted*

Break the marzipan into small pieces and place in a bowl with the icing sugar. Rub the two ingredients together until they resemble fine breadcrumbs. Add the orange rind and Grand Marnier and continue rubbing the mixture until it forms a pliable dough. If, after considerable kneading and rubbing, the mixture does not resemble a dough and is still dry, add a small amount of egg white until the dough is pliable. Cover the dough and allow it to sit for 24 hours so that the flavour of the orange rind and Grand Marnier can penetrate the marzipan.

Roll the marzipan dough on a lightly floured surface to 1 cm (⅓ in) thickness and place on to a sheet of baking parchment. Pour half of the melted chocolate on to the marzipan surface and spread it evenly using a palette knife. Spread it right to the edges. Place the marzipan on to a tray and refrigerate until the chocolate has set firm. Remove from the refrigerator, turn the marzipan slab over and coat the other side with the remaining melted chocolate. Refrigerate again until the chocolate is firm. When the second side has set, trim the edges with a hot knife and cut the slab into small even squares. Be careful not to splinter or crack the chocolate.

Note: These petits fours are very sweet and therefore need to be cut very small.

Makes 18–24

Rout Biscuits

◆

540 g (19 oz) plain marzipan (see note
below, also see p. 61)
1 ½ cups (10 ½ oz) caster (superfine)
sugar
4 egg whites
210 g (7 ½ oz) dark (plain or
semi-sweet) chocolate, melted

Preheat oven to 200°C (400°F). Line
a baking tray (sheet) with baking
parchment.

Place the marzipan and sugar in a
bowl and mix together until they
form a solid mass. Slowly add the egg
whites until a nice piping consistency
is formed. This may take more or less
egg white depending on the brand of
marzipan used. When the mixture is
ready (better too stiff than too runny)
place it into a piping (pastry) bag,
fitted with a 1 ½ cm (½ in) star-
shaped nozzle or a 1 cm (⅓ in) round
plain nozzle. Pipe the mixture on to
the prepared tray in various shapes.
Bake the shapes in the preheated
oven approximately 10–12 minutes.

Once cooked, cool on the tray.
Remove the baking parchment and
dip the bases in the melted chocolate.
When the chocolate is set put the
biscuits in an airtight container and
store them in the freezer. Remove
1 hour before eating to allow them
to defrost.
Note: It is important that you use
the correct type of marzipan (66%
almond, 34% sugar) for these
biscuits.

Makes 36

Rout Biscuits

Marzipan Truffles

Marzipan Truffles

300 g (10 ½ oz) plain marzipan (see p. 61)
½ cup (2 oz) slivered almonds, finely chopped
15 ml (½ fl oz) Amaretto liqueur
300 g (10 ½ oz) dark (plain or semi-sweet) chocolate, melted
1 ⅓ cups (5 oz) flaked almonds, lightly roasted
icing (powdered) sugar, for dusting

Break the marzipan into small pieces and place into a mixing bowl with the finely chopped almonds and the Amaretto liqueur. Rub these ingredients together until the mixture forms a solid mass.

If the dough is slightly sticky add a small amount of icing sugar. Take teaspoons of the dough and roll into balls. Dip the fingers of one hand in the melted chocolate and coat each ball of marzipan in chocolate by rolling it in your hand. Roll the marzipan balls in the lightly roasted almonds to coat.

Place all the marzipan balls on to a tray and refrigerate for several minutes to harden the chocolate. Dust lightly with icing sugar to serve.

Makes 18–24

Modelled Marzipan Fruit and Vegetables

◆

TO TINT OR COLOUR MARZIPAN

When modelling either fruit or vegetables there are two ways of colouring them. The European way is to mould or shape the plain (white or clear) marzipan (see p. 61) into its final form, then allow it to sit and dry out overnight so it forms a skin which will absorb the colours that are painted on later by hand.

The American method is to mould the product from a basic colour suitable to that fruit or vegetable and perfect the colour later by painting in the details.

To create a basic colour marzipan for the American method, flatten the piece of marzipan to be coloured and add a drop of food colouring to the centre. Fold the marzipan to enclose the colouring. Lightly knead the marzipan until the colouring is completely absorbed. Continue to add food colouring drop by drop using the same method until the required colour is achieved.

When you use food colouring to create different-coloured marzipan, be careful not to get it on your clothes as it stains.

Marzipan Bananas

◆

Approximately 300 g (10 ½ oz) of marzipan will make 12 bananas.

Roll a small piece of yellow-tinted marzipan in the palm of your hand until it forms a ball. Roll into a sausage shape. Place slight pressure on one side while rolling to taper the sausage. Bend slightly to resemble a banana. Square off the thickest end by pinching it between three fingers. Use the back of a spoon or knife to smooth the curved surface of the banana. Allow to dry for 1 hour before painting with green food colouring and melted dark (plain or semi-sweet) chocolate.

Marzipan Carrots

◆

Approximately 250 g (9 oz) of marzipan will make 12 carrots.

Roll a small piece of orange-tinted marzipan between the palms of your hands until it forms a ball. Roll back and forth to taper the ball at one end. The narrow end should be short and blunt, not pointed. Place the carrot on a bench (counter) top and use the back of a knife to lightly score marks all over the carrot.

stalk, into the top of the indentation.

To make the pumpkin into a jack-o'-lantern, press 2 triangles of dark brown marzipan into the orange marzipan for the eyes. Mark a jagged mouth with a sharp knife.

Marzipan Pumpkins

◆

Approximately 400 g (14 oz) of marzipan will make 12 pumpkins and their stalks.

Roll a small piece of orange-tinted marzipan into a ball shape. Hold the ball between your thumb and finger and mark five lines around the sides of the ball, going from top to bottom, using the handle of a knife or the side of a pen. Place the balls on to a flat surface and using your thumb press down slightly on the top of each ball to give a slight indent where all the lines have met. Press a little piece of green marzipan, which has been rolled into a sausage shape for the

Marzipan Strawberries

◆

Approximately 200 g (7 oz) of marzipan will make 12 strawberries and their stalks.

Roll a small piece of pink or red-coloured marzipan (coloured with 2–3 drops of red (cochineal) colouring) into a ball shape and then slightly taper one side of the ball by rolling it back and forth between the palm of your hand. It should look like a flat kind of pear.

Press a toothpick into the largest end of the tapered ball to make a small hole. Roll the piece of marzipan gently back and forth over the rough side of a fine grater to give it the markings of a strawberry. Take a small piece of green-coloured marzipan, pinch it into a four pointed star, flatten and attach it to the top of the strawberry.

Marzipan Oranges and Lemons

◆

For both the lemon and the orange, approximately 200 g (7 oz) of marzipan will make 12 of each fruit.

To make an orange, roll a small piece of orange-tinted marzipan into a ball. Roll the ball back and forth over the rough side of a fine grater to give it the texture of an orange. In one side press a clove for the stalk.

To make a lemon, roll a small piece of yellow marzipan into a ball and then roll it between the palms of your hands so that both ends of the

ball are slightly tapered. Roll the piece of marzipan over the rough side of a fine grater to give it the texture of a lemon. Using a toothpick, insert two small holes into both ends of the lemon. Allow the lemon to dry for 1 hour before painting both of the tapered ends slightly with light green food colouring.

Marzipan Cherries

◆

Approximately 150 g (5 oz) of marzipan and 100 g (3 ½ oz) dark (plain or semi-sweet) chocolate will make 12 finished cherries.

Roll two small pieces of red-tinted (cochineal-tinted) marzipan into balls and set them close together on a flat surface. Into the top of each ball press a toothpick to make two small depressions where the stalk will go. On a piece of baking parchment pipe a large 'V' shape of melted dark chocolate. This 'V' should be large enough at the open end to be inserted into the two holes in the red balls. (The chocolate will form the stalk.) Allow the chocolate to set in the refrigerator, then peel it from the paper. Insert the chocolate piece into the top of the balls and press in slightly.

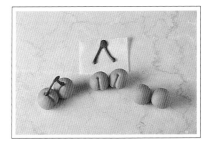

Marzipan Frog

Approximately 120 g (4 oz) of marzipan will make one frog.

Roll 100 g (3 ½ oz) of green-tinted marzipan into a sausage shape approximately 1 ½ cm (½ in) wide and 5 cm (2 in) long. One-third of the way along the sausage place three fingers and roll the marzipan so that three indentations are formed and lengthen the marzipan by 2 cm (¾ in). On the other end of the sausage roll the marzipan so that

there are two indentations stretching the marzipan for 2 cm (¾ in). Cut down the middle of both stretched pieces leaving a whole piece of unrolled sausage shape in the centre. Spread apart the two halves of the longest rolled end and sit the rest of the piece upright. Bend the two long pieces of marzipan up so that they look like bent frog legs and sit either side of the body. Set the two short halves between the legs on the side.

To make the head of the frog take the rest of the green-tinted marzipan and roll it into a ball. Using your thumb, make two large indentations for the eyes at the top of the ball and push out the bottom of the ball for a mouth. Sit the head on top of the body. Using a sharp knife cut the mouth slightly so that it is open. Using melted white chocolate pipe two balls of chocolate into the eye sockets. Dot each eyeball with a little melted dark chocolate.

Marzipan Turtle

Approximately 160 g (5 ½ oz) of marzipan will make one turtle.

Roll 100 g (3 ½ oz) of brown-tinted marzipan into a ball shape. Flatten the ball shape between your hands so that it is quite flat but still rounded on top. Mark the top of the flattened shape so that it resembles a turtle's shell. Roll six 10 g (⅓ oz) shapes of brown-tinted marzipan into balls, then into pear-shaped pieces. Insert one piece under one end of the shell as the tail. Two pieces go on either side of the shell and are slightly flattened on one end for the flippers.

The final piece for the head is inserted under the front of the shell. Use a knife or sharp instrument to mark two holes for eyes and then cut a slit into the lower half for the mouth. Pipe a small dot of melted white chocolate into the two eye holes and use melted dark (plain or semi-sweet) chocolate to pipe on eyebrows and pupils for the eyes.

Marzipan: Lemons, Bananas, Oranges, Cherries and Strawberries

Sugar-glazed Fruit

CHAPTER FOUR

Fruit-based

Fruit has its own natural sweetness and appeal. In this
chapter we experiment with fruit and turn it into
all kinds of wonderful petits fours.

◆

Small fruit such as berries and grapes are a perfect
size for decorating or accompanying petits fours.
Slices of luscious, colourful mandarin, lemon and
even star fruit (carambola) look fabulous when
frosted, glazed with sugar or dipped in chocolate.
Fruit is a versatile and readily available medium for
creating delicious petits fours.

Sugar-glazed Fruit

❖

Encased in a crisp shell of sugar, these petits fours are delightful with coffee or as a light bite throughout the day. Use only the freshest skinned fruit for these delicate morsels and do not make more than is required as the sugar casing will not last if stored.

2 cups (18 oz) white granulated sugar
250 ml (8 ½ fl oz) water
1 tablespoon (1 oz) liquid glucose (corn) syrup
fruit of your choice, washed and dried (perhaps grapes, small berries, fresh cherries or mandarin segments)

Place the sugar, water and glucose in a saucepan and slowly bring to the boil. While the mixture is boiling, brush down the sides of the saucepan with a pastry brush dipped in warm, clean water. This will remove any sugar crystals left on the sides. Boil the mixture to 140°C (290°F) measuring with a sugar (candy) thermometer. Remove immediately from the heat and dip the saucepan into a bowl of cold water for several seconds to prevent any further cooking.

Using a toothpick or fork, lift the fruit and dip each piece of fruit into the sugar mixture. Make certain that you do not pierce the skin of the fruit. If the fruit is pierced the sugar glaze will begin to dissolve. If you are glazing grapes, select a small bunch still joined to a stem. (You will be able to pick them up by the stem.) For mandarin segments lift and dip them using a fork. Be very careful not to splash the syrup on to yourself as it will instantly burn your skin.

Once the fruit is dipped, quickly allow the excess syrup to drain off, then place the fruit on to baking parchment to set hard.

Note: Sugar glazing is the process by which boiling sugar liquid is poured over fruit and then allowed to harden, giving the fruit a solid and protective skin. Strawberries cannot be used in the sugar glazing process as their high water content causes them to boil underneath the glaze. All sugar-glazed fruit must be used the same day. You will need a sugar (candy) thermometer to make the sugar glaze.

Makes 24–30 glazed grapes or fruit of similar size

1. Dip the saucepan into a bowl of cold water for several seconds to prevent any further cooking.

2. Using a toothpick or fork dip each piece of fruit into the sugar mixture.

3. Place the dipped fruit pieces on to baking parchment to set hard.

Chocolate-dipped Fruit

Rather than leaving these petits fours plain, you can serve them in a variety of ways including: dusted with icing (powdered) sugar or dusted with a mixture of icing sugar and cocoa powder.

300 g (10 ½ oz) dark (plain or semi-sweet) chocolate, melted
30 g (1 oz) Copha (white coconut shortening), melted
fruit of your choice, washed and dried (perhaps strawberries, star fruit (carambola), mandarin segments, grapes or cherries)
1 ½ cups (4 oz) sesame seeds, roasted in the oven until slightly brown

Mix the chocolate and Copha together well. Dip the fruits as far as their stalks and allow excess chocolate to drip off. Sit each piece of fruit on a bed of cold, roasted sesame seeds, before placing on to a baking tray (sheet) lined with baking parchment.

When the tray is full place it into the refrigerator to set the chocolate. Serve with coffee or dessert.

Note: As with the sugar-glazed fruits, these should be made and eaten the same day. This is because, even in good storage conditions, the fruit will shrink away from the chocolate casing within 24 hours.

Makes 24–30 dipped strawberries or fruit of similar size

Chocolate-dipped Fruit

Fresh Fruit Kebabs (above), Frosted Fruit (below)

Frosted Fruit

◆

2 egg whites
fresh fruits of your choice, dry and with
a skin (perhaps gooseberries,
strawberries or grapes)
1 cup (7 ½ oz) caster (superfine) sugar

Lightly whisk the egg whites in a small bowl. Dip each piece of fruit into the egg whites separately and very lightly. Allow excess liquid to drain from the fruit so that only a very light coating remains. Roll the fruit immediately into the sugar and place on to a piece of baking parchment to dry. Serve in small paper cups. Do not allow excess egg white to remain on the fruit or place the fruit into the refrigerator. If this is done the sugar will dissolve.

Makes 24 strawberries or fruit of
similar size

Fresh Fruit Kebabs

◆

1 star fruit (carambola)
1 mandarin
1 bunch of grapes
½ pineapple
200 g (7 oz) strawberries
60 ml (2 fl oz) Cointreau or
Grand Marnier
10–12 wooden skewers or cocktail
sticks, approximately 10 cm (4 in) long
icing (powdered) sugar, for dusting

Cut all the fruit except the strawberries into bite-sized pieces. Cut the strawberries in half. Soak the fruit in the liqueur for 1–2 hours. Thread pieces of each fruit on to skewers. Place the kebabs back in the liqueur and dust them lightly with icing sugar before serving to give the fruit a light glaze.

Makes 10–12 kebabs

Fresh Fruit Tartlets

◆

1 ¾ cups (7 ½ oz) plain
(all-purpose) flour
½ cup (3 oz) icing (powdered) sugar
150 g (5 oz) unsalted butter
2 egg yolks

CRÉME CHANTILLY
2 tablespoons (1 oz) icing (powdered)
sugar
2 drops vanilla essence (extract)
300 ml (10 ½ fl oz) thickened
(double or heavy) cream

selection of fresh fruits
extra icing (powdered) sugar, for
dusting

Preheat oven to 180℃ (350°F).
Grease a tartlet pan (12-14 moulds).
Sift the flour and icing sugar into
a bowl. Rub the butter into the dry
ingredients until the mixture
resembles fresh breadcrumbs. Add the
egg yolks and continue mixing until a
dough is formed. Wrap the dough in
plastic (cling) wrap and refrigerate
until firm. Remove the dough and
knead until pliable. On a lightly
floured surface roll the dough to
2 mm or as thin as possible. (Take
care when rolling pastry. It will be
short and may crumble if not worked
carefully.) Using a 4–5 cm (1 ½ –
2 in) plain round cookie cutter, cut
discs from the dough and press them
into the tartlet moulds. Bake in the
preheated oven 12 minutes and then
allow to cool in the pan.

No more than 1 hour prior to
serving, fill each tartlet with a teaspoon of the Créme Chantilly and
garnish with your favourite fruit, cut
into small pieces. Dust lightly with
icing sugar. The fruit will shine from
the glaze created by the icing sugar
mixing with the fruit's natural juice.

CRÉME CHANTILLY
Place the icing sugar and vanilla with
the cream in a small bowl and whisk
until stiff. Do not over-whip as this
will spoil the flavour and texture.

Makes 12–18

Fresh Fruit Tartlets (left), Candied or Mixed Peel (right)

Candied or Mixed Peel

◆

2 oranges
2 lemons
1 cup (8 ½ oz) white granulated
sugar
150 ml (5 fl oz) water
2 tablespoons (2 oz) liquid glucose
(corn) syrup

Make sure that the oranges and lemons have clean skin. Using a sharp knife carefully remove the skin. Try not to take too much of the white pith with it. When all the rind has been removed from the fruit cut away any excess pith from the rind. Cut each of the strips of rind 1–2 mm thick or as thin as possible.

Put the sugar, water and glucose into a saucepan and bring to the boil. Add the rind of the fruit and boil for a further 20 minutes. As the mixture boils, wash down the sides of the saucepan with a pastry brush dipped in warm water. Place the peel on a wire cooling rack and allow to drain and dry overnight. Once dried, the peel can be cut into small pieces and used in cakes or puddings, fondues, dipped in chocolate or eaten by itself.

Makes 1 cup of peel

Important Notes

◆

All ingredients should be at room temperature when used unless the recipe advises otherwise. Ensure that all utensils are clean, dry and grease free before cooking. Water or grease on utensils can adversely affect recipes, especially when using egg whites, which will not reach maximum aeration if mixed with even small amounts of grease or water.

EGG WEIGHTS
All eggs used in these recipes should be 55-60 g (approximately 2 oz).

BAKING TRAY (SHEET) SIZES
In all the recipes we have endeavoured to provide you with international tray sizes but if you find that the tray size suggested is not available please use the closest size you can find. For this reason you may need two trays when we suggest one.

MAKING A PAPER PIPING (PASTRY) BAG
Begin making all piping bags with a triangle-shaped piece of baking parchment. Take the top corner of the paper and roll it along the longest edge. Pinch the point of the roll with one hand and continue rolling the paper with the other. When all of the paper has been rolled, tuck the remaining flap inside the cone. Cut a small point from the end of the bag. If a larger opening is required it is best to begin cutting small pieces from the tip until you attain the required size. If too large a tip is cut the filling may escape too easily. Half fill the bag with mixture for best piping results.

MARZIPAN
Marzipan is a sweetened mixture of ground almonds, liquid glucose (corn) syrup and icing (powdered) sugar. It is also known as almond paste. Marzipan is available in a variety of sizes and packagings.

Marzipan can absorb moisture or dry out so careful storage is essential. If it absorbs moisture it will begin to dissolve. If marzipan dries out it will begin to ferment. To store marzipan, wrap it in plastic (cling) wrap and place it in an airtight container. Store at room temperature in a dark place for up to three weeks.

To bake marzipan it must have a higher proportion of almonds than sugar. If the proportion of sugar is too high, the marzipan will boil instead of bake, which will adversely affect the taste and appearance of the finished creation. The preferred ratio is 66 % almond and 34% sugar.

Chocolate Piping Designs

These chocolate piping designs can be used for decorating the tops of any petit four but they are mostly used for the decoration of Petit Four Glacé. These designs can be piped directly on top of the finished petit four, with a paper (piping) bag (see p. 62) or piped on to baking parchment and allowed to set before removing and placing on top of the petit four.

1. Fill a paper piping bag with chocolate and cut a fine nozzle from the tip.

2. Lightly pipe the chocolate designs on to the baking parchment.

3. Remove set designs from the paper to the food to be decorated.

OVEN TEMPERATURES AND GAS MARKS

◆

DEGREES (F)	200	225	250	275	300	325	350	375	400	425	450
GAS MARK 1	¼	½	1	2	3	4	5	6	7	8	9
GAS MARK 2	1	2	3	4	5	6	7	8	9	10	11

Acknowlegements

◆

The author would like to thank the following people and organisations for their assistance and support:

Gwen Gedeon, from The Welsh Lady Patisserie, for her professional generosity

Brian Cox, General Manager, Socomin International Fine Foods, for their Odense range of products

Paul Frizzel, Account Executive, Sunny Queen Eggs

Anna Permezel, James Tan, Rod Slater and Kay Cafarella of Cadbury Confectionery

Juliet Van Den Heuval, the Prestige Group

J.D. Millner and Associates, for their Le Creuset range of products

Jan Liddle, Glad Products of Australia

The promotions team at Myer Brisbane City Store

Sally Armonoras, Queensco United Dairy Foods

John Reid, Defiance Milling

John Dart, Trumps Nuts and Dried Fruits

Ian Elliot, CSR, for their range of sugar products

Lois Stocks, author of The Home Confectioner

Designer Trim Pty Ltd, Surry Hills, NSW & Richmond, Vic